CRAFTS
for
Revamping
Your Room

written by
Susannah Blake

Enslow Publishers, Inc.
40 Industrial Road
Box 398
Berkeley Heights, NJ 07922
USA

http://www.enslow.com

Library of Congress Cataloging-in-Publication Data
Blake, Susannah.
Crafts for revamping your room / Susannah Blake.
pages cm. — (Eco chic)
Audience: 9-12
Audience: Grade 4 to Grade 6
Summary: "A variety of crafts to redecorate your room using new
and recycled items"—Provided by publisher.
Includes bibliographical references.
ISBN 978-0-7660-4315-2
1. Handicrafts — Juvenile literature. 2. Recyling [Waste, etc.]
3. Gifts — Juvenile literature.
I. Title II. Series
TX 171.883 2013
745.5--dc23
2012025481
Cataloging-in-Publication Data available from the Library of Congress

Future editions:
Paperback ISBN: 978-1-4644-0575-4

To Our Readers: We have done our best to make sure all Internet
addresses in this book were active and appropriate when we went to
press. However, the author and the publisher have no control over
and assume no liability for the material available on those Internet
sites or on other Web sites they may link to. Any comments or
suggestions can be sent by e-mail to comments@enslow.com or to
the address on the back cover.

Printed in China
122012 WKT, Shenzhen, Guangdong, China
10 9 8 7 6 5 4 3 2 1

First published in the UK in 2012 by Wayland
Copyright © Wayland 2012
Wayland
338 Euston Rd
London NW1 3BH

Editors: Julia Adams; Katie Woolley
Craft stylist: Annalees Lim
Designer: Rocket Design (East Anglia) Ltd
Photographer: Simon Pask, N1 Studios

Wayland is a division of Hachette Children's Books,
an Hachette UK company.
www.hachette.co.uk

Picture acknowledgements:
All step-by-step and craft photography: Simon Pask, N1 Studios;
images used throughout for creative graphics: Shutterstock.com

Dear diary
Page 8

Nightstand
Page 16

Contents

SAFETY ADVICE
When you make any of the projects in this book, always put safety first. Be extremely careful with sharp scissors, needles, and pins and ask an adult if you need any help.

Learn stitches Page 30

Beanbag bookends Page 6

Bedroom makeover

All these fab crafts are made f
stuff that usually gets thrown

The world of interior design is a fickle thing, with yesterday's must-have becoming today's throwaway. But it needn't be that way! This book shows you the art of upcycling by using clever tricks to transform something old into something stylish and new.

Dapper decorations and fashionable furnishings

From bunting, door signs, and wall art to cushions, bookends, and doorstops, there's no end to the bedroom accessories that you can make from recycled materials. Reuse fabrics from old clothes, bedding, and curtains. Reclaim beads and baubles from broken or discarded jewelry, snip buttons and sequins off old clothes, save ribbons from gifts and packaging, and use leftover wool from knitting projects or an unraveled sweater or scarf. Set aside decorative paper such as used wrapping paper, magazines, newspapers, and stationery that you could recycle and use to decorate projects.

As well as being great for your room
the crafts in this book make super pres

Funky furniture

Furniture that is perfect for reclaiming, renovating, and revamping is all too often thrown on the landfill heap and rejected in favor of something brand new. So stop that trend and make it work for you! Furniture can be repainted or refreshed and decorated with scrap paper (see page 17). An old armchair or sofa can be covered with a pretty throw. And simply redressing an old bed with a bright quilt and funky cushions can transform a bedroom.

You may have furniture already that you can bring back to life with some clever crafting, but if you don't, there are lots of places to search out pre-loved pieces. Start off by looking in rummage sales, thrift stores, and secondhand furniture stores. The Internet can also be a great source with Web sites where you can look for local goods that are no longer wanted and Web sites where you can pick up furniture very cheaply in an online auction. In all cases, make sure you have an adult's permission and help in obtaining furniture.

Don't be trashy – recycle!

5

Beanbag bookends

Keep your books in order with these funky beanbag bookends! You can make the beanbags using fabric from old clothes, and decorate them with reclaimed ribbons and buttons. You can use a bag of rice, lentils, or dried beans that are out of date and no good for cooking. They're ideal for filling the beanbags.

1 Cut out twelve 4 x 4-inch squares from the sturdy fabric.

2 Cut out shapes, such as hearts or butterflies, from the denim or any other fabric you may have. Sew the shapes on to at least two of the squares, along with ribbons and buttons to decorate.

3

Choose six squares for each bookend. Lay four of the squares in a row and place a square on each side of the strip to make a cross shape. Then flip each square so that the back of the fabric is showing.

4

Use a running stitch (see page 30) to sew the edges of the squares together. Leave an inch open on the final seam.

5

Turn the cube inside out so that all the seams are on the inside. Then use a funnel to fill with beans, lentils, or grains.

Sew up the final seam, tucking the edges in.

The more squares you decorate, the more different looks you can create. Simply rotate the bookends each day to find the design that suits your mood!

Dear diary...

Create your very own personal journal that fastens shut with a clever button and ribbon tie to keep your secrets safe. Collect unused scrap paper that's suitable for writing on for the inside pages, such as envelopes, colored wrapping paper, and old packaging. Scraps of fabric or felt from old clothes are ideal for decorating the cover.

You will need

* scissors
* cardboard from a cereal box
* sturdy fabric or denim
* scraps of fabric or felt, ribbons, and buttons to decorate
* needle and thread
* fabric glue
* plain scrap paper
* hole punch
* button(s) and ribbon to fasten the diary with

1 Cut the cardboard into two 9 x 12-inch rectangles. Then cut out two 10 x 13-inch pieces of sturdy fabric. Sew scraps of fabric, ribbons, and buttons onto one of them to decorate. Sew a large button (or two on top of each other) on the right-hand side of the decorated cover.

2 Use fabric glue to stick each piece of fabric to a cardboard rectangle, folding the fabric over to make a neat edge. Leave to dry completely. Then stick a smaller rectangle of cardboard on to cover the glued edges.

Paper recycling

Even though paper is easily recycled, much of it ends up in landfills. What many people don't realize is that paper can take between five and fifteen years to break down.

As the paper decomposes in landfills it can create methane gas, which is highly combustible and dangerous.

3

Cut the scrap paper into 6 x 8-inch rectangles, then stack them neatly. Working with a few pieces of paper at a time, punch six holes along one edge. Make sure that the holes are in the same position on all the pieces of paper.

4

Insert the pages between the front and back cover, ensuring the holes match up. Sew through the cardboard and the holes in the paper to bind the book together.

5

Tie a ribbon around the book and fasten it into place by looping it around the button.

Use a thread color that contrasts nicely with the color of the cover.

You can reuse this diary over and over again—just cut the thread, replace the pages, and sew everything back together.

9

Personalized door sign

Let everyone know who sleeps here with this funky personalized door sign! You only need a DVD case, photos, and scrap paper. Be super chic by choosing colors that match your bedroom décor.

1 Remove the original paper sleeve from the DVD case. Use it as a template to cut out a piece of scrap paper that is slightly smaller, and one that is the same size.

2 Decorate the smaller piece of paper with shapes cut out of scrap paper. Alternatively, you might want to make a collage with photos of family and friends, or a big picture of yourself with some pretty shapes. When you are finished decorating, stick this piece of paper onto the one that is the same size as the DVD sleeve.

Recycling photographs

Photographic paper can't be recycled like other paper products. The chemicals used in the paper and thin layer of polythene that coats the photo clog up the recycling process at paper mills.

Although this is bad news in one way, it gives you loads of opportunities to be really creative in making the most of your photos in projects such as this one.

Slide this new sleeve into the DVD case, then lay the string or ribbon along the spine. Snap the case shut and tie the ends of the string or ribbon together to make a hanging loop.

It's amazing what you can find lying around. We even used an old map for these heart shapes!

If you decide to cut up some of your old photos, make sure you ask a grown-up first—he or she might like to keep them!

Hang the sign on your bedroom door!

Pretty as a picture

Finding a picture frame

If you don't have a picture frame at home, look out for one in thrift stores and rummage sales. They're a great place to hunt out pre-loved items for you to recycle and revamp and usually cost very little.

Become an artist and create your very own artwork for your bedroom. Take an old picture frame and create a brand-new picture to go inside it using scrap paper, such as graph paper, old envelopes, magazines, and newspapers.

You will need

★ sandpaper (optional)
★ acrylic paint
★ paintbrush
★ scrap paper, buttons
★ glue
★ scissors
★ cardboard from a cereal box

1

Carefully remove the back and glass from the picture frame. You may want to sand the frame to make the paint stick to it well. Then paint with acrylic paint and leave to dry.

2

Cut out a piece of paper to fit inside the frame. Create a collage picture by gluing shapes on top, leaving plenty of space around the outside for a mount.

3

To make a mount, cut out a piece of cardboard the same size as the picture. Mark a rectangle inside leaving a border of at least one inch. Cut out the center to create the mount.

Paint the mount in a color that goes well with those used in the picture. Set it aside to dry.

Place the mount on the picture, then slip into the frame and clip back together. Hang it on your bedroom wall!

Buttoned wool cushion

This project is a fantastic way to give a new lease of life to an old cardigan. The buttoned front gives a stylish finish with almost no effort at all! Use an old cushion or cushion pad for the filling.

You will need

★ an old buttoned cardigan
★ cushion pad
★ dress-making pins
★ scissors
★ needle and thread

1 Turn the cardigan inside out and lay it flat on a table. Place the cushion pad on the cardigan and mark its shape using dress-making pins.

2 Cut around the pins to make the basic cushion shape. Make sure you leave a border around the pins of about one inch.

Never throw your worn-out sweaters away. Even if they have holes you can still recycle the fabric.

Using a running stitch (see page 30), sew all the way around the edge of the pins. Repeat to give a double layer of extra-strong stitches.

Unbutton the front of the cardigan and turn it the right way round, so that the seams are inside. Insert the cushion and button up to create the finished cushion!

You can even replace the buttons to give the cushions a more stylish look.

Disposable fashion

The fads of fashion contribute a million tons of waste to landfills every year, so it's a great idea to recycle old clothes in any way you can.

Many old clothes are perfect for transforming into soft furnishings.

Use your imagination and see what else you can find to turn yesterday's style statement into today's chic interior!

These cardigans had pockets. On a cushion, they are great for storing knick-knacks.

15

Nightstand

Upcycle your tired old nightstand and turn it into the centerpiece of your room! All you need is a little paint and some scrap paper. Search out colored scrap paper such as magazines, newspapers, junk mail, leaflets, and flyers that will complement the other colors in your bedroom. Before you start, check that you are allowed to renovate the nightstand!

You will need
★ sandpaper (optional)
★ nightstand
★ acrylic paint
★ paintbrush
★ scissors
★ scrap paper
★ PVA glue

1

If necessary, lightly sand the nightstand to help the paint stick to the surface. Then paint with acrylic paint and leave to dry.

2

Cut the scrap paper into shapes. You might want to use them to create a little scene or a colorful collage.

The paint will cover better if you use a lighter shade of paint as an undercoat. Perhaps you have some that needs using up?

When the nightstand is completely dry, stick the shapes on in your chosen design using PVA glue.

Paint a thin layer of PVA glue over the whole nighstand to seal your design and leave to dry completely.

We painted this nightstand using paint samples. You can get these for free or very little money in DIY stores.

17

Bunting!

Nothing cheers up a bedroom like a string of bunting! Whether it's in bright colors or seaside stripes, bunting is a great way to add a touch of fun to your room. Pick out some old clothes that don't fit you anymore so that you can turn happy memories into funky interior fashion.

You will need

★ an old pair of jeans
★ scrap material from old clothes
★ ribbon or string
★ scissors
★ needle and thread

1 Cut the jeans into triangles (about 10 in. high and 8 in. wide). You will need at least five triangles, and it is ideal to end up with an odd, rather than an even, number.

10 in.

2 Cut out shapes or letters from the scrap material. You can make their edges look pretty by adding a blanket stitch (see page 31).

Sew the shapes onto the triangles. If you have beads, you can attach them to the bottom of each triangle.

Sew the top of each triangle to the ribbon with about one inch between each one. If you only have short bits of ribbon, sew them together to make one long piece before attaching the triangles.

Broken beads

If you break a necklace or bracelet, don't despair. Pick up the beads and store them in a jar. They'll be great for adding decoration to bunting or similar furnishings, such as cushions or mobiles.

Hang the bunting up around your bedroom!

You can personalize your bunting by spelling your name across it!

19

Box of treasures

You will need

★ shoe box
★ PVA glue
★ scissors
★ colorful scrap paper, such as wrapping paper, leftover wallpaper, or magazines
★ small cardboard boxes from food packaging
★ ribbon

Whether you need a jewelry box to keep your beads and bangles in, or just a special place to store your favorite things, this beautiful box is a must for every bedroom.

1

Coat the lid of the shoe box in a thin layer of PVA glue and cover with strips of scrap paper. Leave to dry completely.

If you don't have any colored or patterned paper, you can try cutting up magazines.

2

Place the small cardboard boxes inside the shoe box to create compartments within the box. If necessary, cut down the height of the boxes so that they fit inside the shoe box.

Repackage your packaging

Food and consumer goods create a vast amount of waste due to packaging. Often goods are contained within several layers of packaging. This may be to protect the product on its long journey to the consumer, but these numerous layers of packaging also find their way to the growing heaps of landfills. How many different ways can you think of to reclaim and reuse this excess packaging?

4

Use the ribbon to wrap around the box and fasten it shut.

3

Use the scrap paper to decorate the boxes. Then stick them inside the shoe box.

make these cute butterflies, just layer butterfly shapes in different sizes and colors and stick their center to the box.

can use your box to collect fabric, buttons, and ribbons that you might like to use for other projects.

21

Cute CD hanger

Damaged or used CDs are a tricky thing to recycle, but with their shiny, reflective appearance there are loads of ways you can use them to glam up everyday objects. This cute hanger will add a bit of sparkle to any bedroom!

You will need

- ★ 5-7 old CDs
- ★ scrap paper or magazines
- ★ pencil
- ★ scissors
- ★ glue
- ★ ribbon
- ★ sticky tape
- ★ beads

1 Using a CD as a template, draw circles on the backs of scrap paper or magazine images and cut them out.

2 Cut out pretty flower shapes and stick them onto the circles.

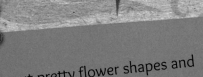

3

Stick the decorated circles onto the CDs.

4

dd beads to one end f the ribbon and tie a not. If you only have hort pieces of ribbon, se a needle and hread to sew them ogether to make a piece long enough for your CDs.

5

Make a loop at the other end of the ribbon, then stick the ribbon to the backs of the CDs with sticky tape. Now it's ready to hang up!

Why not have pictures of your best friends in the center of your CD flowers?

Window mobile

Take nature as your inspiration to make this beautiful leafy mobile. Watch the leaves spin in the breeze and reflect the sunshine on their shiny surface. At night they will shine in the glow of the lightbulb in your bedroom lamp.

You will need

- ★ yarn or embroidery thread
- ★ CD
- ★ images taken from old magazines or scrap paper
- ★ sticky tape
- ★ scissors
- ★ hole punch

1

Wind wool or embroidery thread around the CD to cover the shiny surface.

Making the most of old CDs

Pass CDs on to someone else who might enjoy them, or give them to a thrift store. Sell them at a rummage sale or hang an ad in your local grocery store. Alternatively, these shining discs make great bird scarers when hung over your veggie patch or in fruit trees. Whatever you do, don't just throw them away—look for a new home or use for them.

Cut the scrap paper into leaf shapes. You can make them all kinds of different shapes and sizes.

People throw away lots of old CDs. If you haven't got any yourself, ask around!

Carefully cover both sides of each leaf with sticky tape. Snip away any excess tape.

If you use tissue paper for your leaves, the light will shine through them like stained glass.

ing the hole
nch, stamp a
le in the top of
ch leaf. Then
tach each of
em to a piece
f yarn or
mbroidery
hread.

Attach the leaves to the CD using a slightly longer piece of wool or thread for each one. Fix four equal lengths of wool to the top of the CD and knot the ends together to hang up your mobile.

Owl doorstop

Make this cute owl doorstop to keep your door open . . . or closed! Use an old pillowcase or fabric from a shirt, dress, or skirt. If you like dressmaking or sewing, you may have some suitable scraps left over from a previous project. An old cushion or puffy jacket are ideal sources of stuffing.

2

Cut out shapes from scrap fabric to make the background for the face, the eyes, the beak, and the feathers. Sew the shapes onto the front of the pillowcase and add two (or four) buttons for the eyes.

1

Cut the pillowcase in half and save the closed end. You can use the open end for another project.

3

Fill the bottom of the pillowcase with a layer of lentils, rice, or dried beans, then fill the rest with stuffing. Sew across the top to enclose the filling materials.

4

Tie the two top corners using some thread to create ears.

Make the most of your kitchen cupboard

If you don't keep track of your kitchen cupboard staples such as couscous, lentils, or rice, you can easily find that a packet has gone past its sell-by date.
Rather than throwing it away, why not use the old grains or seeds for craft projects like this one?

5

Depending on the design of the cushion cover you have, you could make a dog, a cat, or any other animal to guard your door!

You can also make mini owls out of the leftover cushion cover to use as paperweights.

Style your bedroom!

Transforming your room by using new accessories and color is one of the best ways of expressing yourself. And the good news is, it doesn't need to be wasteful or contribute to the ever-growing mountains of landfills. By recycling, reclaiming, and reusing you can make everything out of nothing and give a new lease of life to items that might otherwise have ended up in the garbage.

Embrace your own interior style

Once you've decided what you need, think about color and the kind of accessories and furniture you like. Have the confidence in your own likes and dislikes and create a look that's true to your own taste and style. Think about colors you like and reclaim, recycle, and reuse materials in those shades to create a coordinated look. Or if you prefer a hodgepodge of color and pattern, embrace your quirky side and go for it!

Make it all about you

Before you start on any makeover, think about what you like and what you're like! Are you a girly girl who likes everything pretty and pink, are you a tomboy who loves sports and the outdoors, are you crazy for nature, or do you love reading and studying hard at school?

Once you've decided on these basics, think about what kind of bedroom accessories you need. Do you need a desk for doing homework? Do you need a dressing table for trying out new hairstyles? Do you need bookends to keep your books in order and a diary to write down all your personal thoughts? Do you need cushions and beanbag chairs to hang out on with your friends?

This box of treasures looks fab but there are so many other ways you could decorate it—paint, foils, or even glitter!

28

Reuse your skills

nce you've mastered the basic projects in
s book, think about how you could reuse
ose skills for new projects. Redecorate
her items of furniture using the techniques
ed for the nightstand on pages 16—17,
make a notebook in the same way as
e diary on pages 8—9. You could also
ake a selection of cushions similar to the
e on pages 14—15 using other clothes
th fastenings, such as a zip-up top or a
ttoned shirt.

*The only limit to
restyling your room
is your imagination!*

29

Craft skills

How to thread a needle

Cut a length of thread. Make sure it is no longer than your arm; too long a piece of thread will become knotted and make sewing hard work. Pass the tip of the thread through the eye of the needle. If the ends are frayed, dampen them slightly. Hold the two ends of thread together and loop into a knot. Doubling up the thread will help to make your sewing stronger.

Starting and finishing a line of stitching

To start, fasten the thread to the fabric using a few backstitches. End a line of tacking with one backstitch or a knot.

Sewing on buttons

Buttons usually have two or four holes, or have a single loop underneath. They need to be sewn on very firmly with plenty of stitches as they are generally subject to lots of wear and tear.

For a two-hole or looped button, sew through the holes or loop on to the fabric about six times in the same direction. Tie off on the underside of the fabric. For a four-hole button, use the same technique as for the two-hole button, using opposite holes to make a cross pattern.

Tacking stitch

This is used to hold the fabric in position while it is being permanently stitched and is ideal for gathering fabric into ruffles. Pass the needle in and out of the fabric in a line to make long, even stitches.

To make ruffles, do not tie off the line of stitching, Gently pull the thread, sliding the fabric together into gathers or ruffles. When you have created the desired effect, tie off with a backstitch or knot.

Running stitch

Similar to the tacking stitch, the running stitch uses smaller stitches. It is used for seams and for gathering and can also be used for decorative effect, particularly with wool or embroidery thread. You can stitch lines or curling patterns onto the surface of fabric.

Pass the needle in and out of the fabric in small, even stitches.

Whipstitch

This stitch is used to secure two pieces of fabric together at the edges.

Place two pieces of fabric on top of each other.

Fasten the thread to the inside of one piece of fabric. Pass the needle through both pieces of fabric from underneath, passing through where you have fastened the thread. Stitch through from the underside again to make a diagonal stitch about half an inch from the first stitch.

Blanket stitch

This is a decorative stitch used to bind the edge of fabric. Use a contrasting colored thread for maximum effect.

Fasten the thread on the underside of the fabric, then pass the needle from the underside. Make a looped stitch over the edge of the fabric but before you pull it tight, pass the needle through the loop. Repeat.

Glossary

accessory: A fashion item such as jewelry, a scarf, or a bag that can be added to enhance your overall fashion look.

biodegradable: Materials or substances that can be decomposed by natural bacteria.

consumer: A person who buys products and services for personal use.

contaminant: A toxic or poisonous substance that infects or dirties other substances.

decompose: The process by which man-made and natural materials and substances break down. It can be another word for rotting.

eco: Short for ecology; sometimes used in front of words to imply a positive effect on the environment, for example "eco fashion."

environment: The natural world, including air, soil, water, plants, and animals.

landfill: Also known as a dump, a landfill is a site used for the disposal of waste materials.

organic: Plants and animals that are grown or reared entirely naturally without the use of synthetic inputs such as pesticides, fertilizers, and antibiotics.

pesticide: A chemical used to prevent, destroy, or repel pests.

pollution: The release of environmental contaminants.

recycle: To use something again, usually after processing or remaking in some way.

toxic: Poisonous.

trend: Popular fashion or style at a given time.

upcycle: To take something that is disposable and transform it into something of greater use and value.

Useful Web sites

freecycle.org: A Web site helping to keep unwanted consumer goods out of landfills. It brings together people who want to get rid of things and people who need those things.

etsy.com: A Web site where people can buy and sell handmade crafts. A great source for craft inspiration.

folksy.com: A Web site where people can buy, sell, and learn how to make handmade crafts.

Index